FOREWORD

This book consists only of pieces of the highest musical standards. It is designed for teachers and performers. both professional and amateur, who demand the best material available.

This collection of pieces by great composers has been selected very carefully. It consists of compositions of easy to medium difficulty, almost all of which have been written for the flute. The few which are not (and one can only regret it) have been adapted for the flute because they lie so well for the instrument and are so enjoyable to perform. Great care has been taken in the placement of these pieces. They have been set in progressive order of difficulty. The variety given by key, time, mood and speed has been kept constantly in mind.

The realization of the figured basses of numbers 1, 4, 5, 6, 7 and 20 retains the spirit of the pieces, but breaks away from the traditional chordal writing generally used by arrangers of music of the XVII and XVIII centuries. At that time, the realization of figured basses was left to the performer's imagination and musical ability. It is our conviction that keyboard music demanding realization should not be considered as a mere accompaniment but as a real partner to the solo instrument. We, therefore, have realized the bass in a free way, thus making the right hand part more interesting, while still being strictly respectful of the suggested figured harmonies. We also want to point out that we have chosen the articulations and dynamics that match as closely as possible the style of the composer; but at the same time we have adapted them to the modern possibilities of the instrument.

Louis Moyse

CONTENTS
(in progressive order)

SOLOS
for the
FLUTE
PLAYER

With Piano Accompaniment

Selected and Edited by

LOUIS MOYSE

Ed. 2411

G. SCHIRMER, Inc.

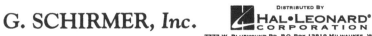
DISTRIBUTED BY
HAL•LEONARD®
CORPORATION
7777 W. BLUEMOUND RD. P.O. BOX 13819 MILWAUKEE, WI 53213

Index by Composers

1. Allegro

(from Sonata for Flute and Piano)

JEAN BAPTISTE LOEILLET (1680-1730)

2. Allegretto

(from Menuetto in F)
(12 Little Pieces for Piano)

JOSEPH HAYDN (1732-1809)

Ländler Tempo

3. Song Without Words

FELIX MENDELSSOHN Op. 62, No. 25
(1809 -1847)

4. Two Menuets

(from Sonata for Flute and Piano)

Menuet I
Dolce con gracia

JEAN-JACQUES NAUDOT (?-1762)

Menuet II

D.C. Menuet I al Fine

D.C. Menuet I al Fine

5. Gavotte

(from Sonata for Flute and Piano)

GEORGE FRIDERIC HANDEL (1685-1759)

6. Andante and Allegretto

(from Sonata for Flute and Piano)

GENERAL JOHN REID (1721-1807)

7. Two Arias in Rondeau

(from Sonata for Flute and Piano)

JEAN-JACQUES NAUDOT (?-1762)

Air II

23

Air I

8. Rosamunde

(Ballet Music)

FRANZ SCHUBERT (1797-1828)

9. Air

(from L'Apothéose de Lulli)

FRANÇOIS COUPERIN (1668-1733)

Gracieusement

10. Polonaise

(from Sonata for Flute and Piano)

LUDWIG VAN BEETHOVEN (1770-1827)

SOLOS
for the
FLUTE
PLAYER

With Piano Accompaniment

Selected and Edited by

LOUIS MOYSE

Ed. 2411

G. SCHIRMER, Inc.

DISTRIBUTED BY
HAL•LEONARD®
CORPORATION
7777 W. BLUEMOUND RD PO BOX 13819 MILWAUKEE, WI 53213

MMO 111 SOLOS FOR THE FLUTE PLAYER

Cue Sheet

Allegro	3 taps (1 measure)
Allegretto	5 taps (1 2 3 / 1 2)
Song Without Words	4 taps (1 measure)
Two Menuets	3 taps (1 measure)
Gavotte	6 taps (1 measure)
Andante & Allegretto	3 taps (1 measure)
Two Airs in Rondeau	3 taps (1 measure)
Rosamunde	No taps needed. (last repeat not taken)
Air	3 taps (1 measure)
Polonaise	No taps needed. (omit 2nd and 3rd repeat)
May, Sweet May	4 taps (2 measures)
Trio des Ismaelites	4 loud taps/8 soft taps (3 meas.) begin on 2nd.
Nocturne	4 taps (1 measure)
Entr'acte	No taps needed.
Adagio	3 taps (1 measure)
Two Passepieds	5 taps (1 2 3/1 2 begin/ only 1st repeat of each Passepied is taken.
Scherzando	4 taps (2 measures)
Adagio	6 taps (1 measure)

Note: May we suggest that the player mark each selection with the appropriate cue to facilitate use of the book, without constant referral to this page.

CONTENTS

(in progressive order)

1. Allegro

(from Sonata for Flute and Piano)

JEAN BAPTISTE LOEILLET (1680-1730)

2. Allegretto

(from Menuetto in F)
(12 Little Pieces for Piano)

FLUTE

JOSEPH HAYDN (1732 -1809)

3. Song Without Words

FELIX MENDELSSOHN Op. 62, No. 25
(1809 - 1847)

FLUTE

FLUTE

4. Two Menuets

(from Sonata for Flute and Piano)

JEAN-JACQUES NAUDOT (?-1762)

5. Gavotte

(from Sonata for Flute and Piano)

GEORGE FRIDERIC HANDEL (1685-1759)

FLUTE

6. Andante and Allegretto

(from Sonata for Flute and Piano)

FLUTE

GENERAL JOHN REID (1721-1807)

FLUTE

7. Two Arias in Rondeau

(from Sonata for Flute and Piano)

JEAN-JACQUES NAUDOT (?-1762)

FLUTE

8. Rosamunde

(Ballet Music)

FLUTE

FRANZ SCHUBERT (1797-1828)

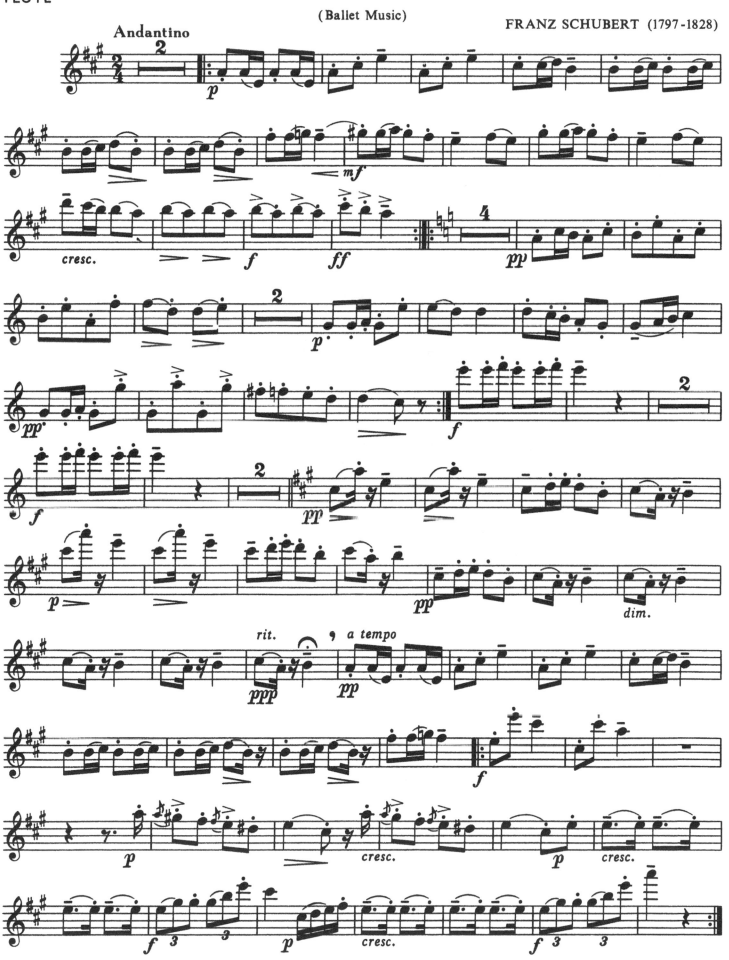

9. Air

(from L'Apothéose de Lulli)

FRANÇOIS COUPERIN (1668 - 1733)

FLUTE

10. Polonaise

(from Sonata for Flute and Piano)

LUDWIG VAN BEETHOVEN (1770-1827)

FLUTE

11. May, Sweet May

(from Album for the Young, op. 68)

FLUTE

ROBERT SCHUMANN (1810–1856)

12. Trio des Ismaelites

(from The Childhood of Christ)

HECTOR BERLIOZ (1803-1869)

FLUTE

FLUTE

13. Nocturne

FLUTE

FRÉDÉRIC CHOPIN Op. 32, No. 1
(1810-1849),

14. Entr'acte

(from Carmen)

FLUTE

GEORGES BIZET (1838-1875)

15. Adagio

(from Flute Quartet, K. 285)

WOLFGANG AMADEUS MOZART (1756-1791)

FLUTE

16. Two Passepieds

(from Partita in B minor for Piano)

FLUTE

JOHANN SEBASTIAN BACH (1685-1750)

FLUTE

17. Scherzando

(from Trio Sonata for Flute, Violin and Piano)

GEORG PHILIPP TELEMANN (1681-1767)

FLUTE

18. Adagio

(from: Symphony No. 24)

FLUTE

JOSEPH HAYDN (1732-1809)

FLUTE

19. Valse-Menuet

(from L'Arlésienne Suite No. 1)

FLUTE

GEORGES BIZET (1838-1875)

FLUTE

20. Rondo
(from Piano Sonata, K. 279)

WOLFGANG AMADEUS MOZART (1756-1791)

21. Allegro

(from Sonata for Flute and Piano)

LEONARDO VINCI (1690-1734)

FLUTE

FLUTE

11. May, Sweet May

(from Album for the Young, op. 68)

ROBERT SCHUMANN (1810-1856)

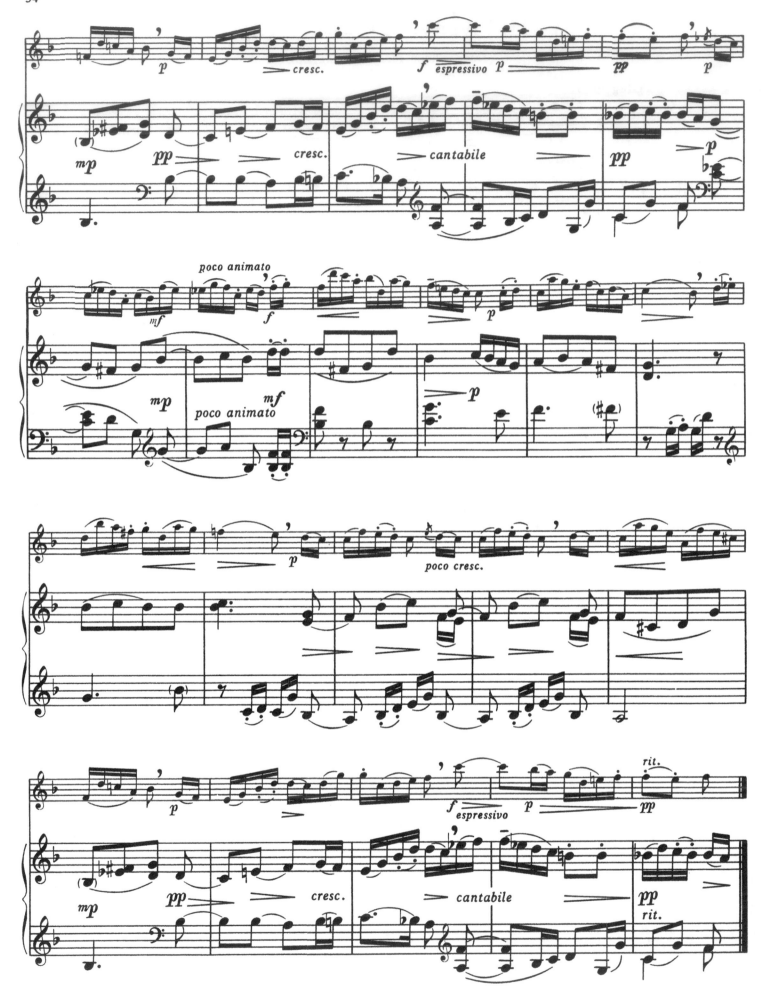

12. Trio des Ismaelites

(from The Childhood of Christ)

HECTOR BERLIOZ (1803-1869)

13. Nocturne

FRÉDÉRIC CHOPIN Op. 32, No. 1
(1810-1849),

14. Entr'acte

(from Carmen)

GEORGES BIZET (1838-1875)

Andantino quasi Allegretto

15. Adagio

(from Flute Quartet, K. 285)

WOLFGANG AMADEUS MOZART (1756-1791)

16. Two Passepieds

(from Partita in B minor for Piano)

JOHANN SEBASTIAN BACH (1685 - 1750)

Passepied II

17. Scherzando

(from Trio Sonata for Flute, Violin and Piano)

GEORG PHILIPP TELEMANN (1681–1767)

18. Adagio

(from: Symphony No.24)

JOSEPH HAYDN (1732-1809)

19. Valse-Menuet

(from L'Arlésienne Suite No.1)

GEORGES BIZET (1838-1875)

Allegro giocoso

20. Rondo

(from Piano Sonata, K. 279)

WOLFGANG AMADEUS MOZART (1756-1791)

21. Allegro

(from Sonata for Flute and Piano)

LEONARDO VINCI (1690 - 1734)